IMAGES
of Sport

SCARBOROUGH
FOOTBALL CLUB

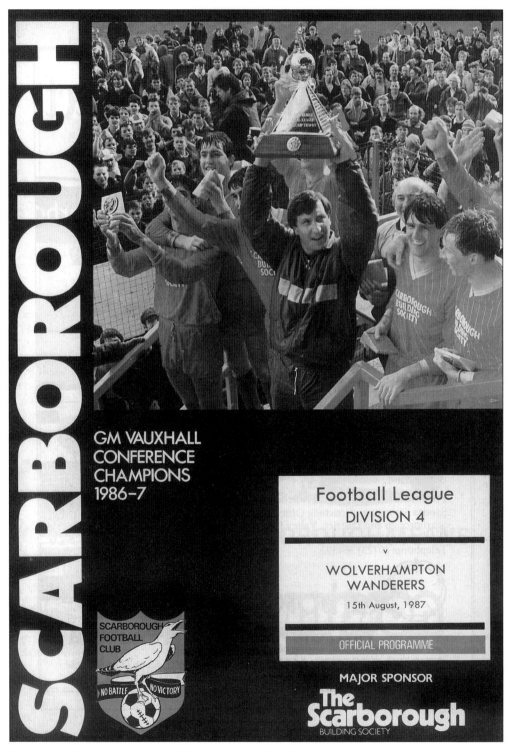

GM VAUXHALL
CONFERENCE
CHAMPIONS
1986–7

SCARBOROUGH
FOOTBALL
CLUB

NO BATTLE — NO VICTORY

Football League
DIVISION 4

v

WOLVERHAMPTON
WANDERERS

15th August, 1987

OFFICIAL PROGRAMME

MAJOR SPONSOR

The
Scarborough
BUILDING SOCIETY

Programme for the match against Wolverhampton Wanderers on 15 August 1987 – Scarborough's first game in the Football League.

IMAGES
of Sport

SCARBOROUGH
FOOTBALL CLUB

Paul Eade

TEMPUS

First published 2002

Tempus Publishing Limited
The Mill, Brimscombe Port,
Stroud, Gloucestershire, GL5 2QG

British Library Cataloguing in Publication Data.
A catalogue record for this book is available from the British Library.

ISBN 0 7524 2426 2

Typesetting and origination by Tempus Publishing Limited
Printed in Great Britain by Midway Colour Print, Wiltshire

Contents

Paul Eade was born in Scarborough and cut his teeth in sports writing as a freelance journalist from 1986 to 1987. From 1988 to 1993 he worked for the *Racing Post* in London before moving on to Press Association Sport in Leeds in 1993. In 1999 he emigrated to Stockholm and returned to freelancing, contributing to numerous football and sports websites in Sweden. *Images of Sport: Scarborough Football Club* is his first book.

Acknowledgements

This book would have been impossible to compile without the co-operation of the Scarborough Evening News. In particular I must thank their Sports Editor, Charles Place, for his advice and support. Another major source was the private collection of Steve Adamson, author of the Official History of Scarborough Football Club and former matchday programme editor. I was particularly grateful to former coach Norman Wardell for responding to my appeal for material and to the contributions made by Peter Elliker, Keith Watson and Bernard Shannon. I also must thank my father for helping me with the collection of materials. In respect of all material, every effort has been made to trace the owner of same, and apologies are offered should copyright have inadvertently been infringed.

Introduction

When I first set out to compile this book in November 2001, there was considerable doubt in my mind whether or not Scarborough Football Club would still exist when it came to publication. At that time the side was rooted to the bottom of the Nationwide Conference, had a scratch squad and was seemingly on the brink of financial oblivion. Subsequent events proved most heartening; the consortium headed by Malcolm Reynolds that effectively saved the club; the appointment of Russell Slade as manager and the side's Lazarus-like rise from the foot of the table to safety by the end of the 2001/02 season.

It is fitting that this book should appear with a new mood of optimism at the club, since Scarborough's recent history has, in the main, been successful. The roots of Scarborough's ascendancy to Football League status in 1987 can be traced back to the early 1960s, when player-manager Eddy Brown produced a successful Midland League side noted for attacking football. In 1963 Scarborough gained five votes – the highest of the twelve clubs putting their names forward – when they applied for election to the Football League.

The next major steps forward came in the 1970s when Scarborough made four FA Trophy final appearances – three of them on the winning side – at Wembley, combined with a string of top five finishes in the Northern Premier League and numerous FA Cup runs, twice reaching the third round proper.

By the time Scarborough entered the newly formed Alliance Premier League in 1979, they were therefore widely acknowledged as one the country's leading non-League clubs.

The early- and mid-1980s could be dubbed the calm before the storm, since Scarborough settled into relative anonymity in their new division (subsequently re-named the Gola League and then GM Vauxhall Conference) before the extraordinary 1986/87 season when an remarkable 22-match unbeaten run pushed them to the top of the table and, on 29 April 1987, to the title. That title brought with it the prize of Football League status as Scarborough became the first ever club to gain automatic promotion to the Football League.

What does the benefit of hindsight tell us about Scarborough's twelve years in the Football League? Things started brightly in terms of both performances on the pitch and attendance figures and in 1989 Boro even looked fit for another promotion. However, once the honeymoon period wore off it became clear that Scarborough was going to struggle to sustain a Football League side when the going got tough. Crowd levels had often been in three figures during the 1980s and when Scarborough's true hardcore support was exposed to be around 1,200-1,300 during the mid-1990s, the maths did not really add up. It was a classic football vicious circle – without money, the club could not afford quality players and without quality players the club could not achieve success and make sufficient money. A brief resurgence did occur in 1997/98, when Scarborough made the Division Three play-offs – but the price to pay was heavy. The club could not continue to pay high wage earners forever and 1998/99 – regardless of the bitter struggles that went on behind the scenes – was always going to be a difficult season.

So, Scarborough went back from whence they came. Lean times followed as the club came to terms with its loss of Football League status, but the opening months of the 2001/02 season were surely the nadir. Now Scarborough Football Club can hold its head proud again. Will there be a second bite of the Football League cherry – indeed, should there be? Or are the lines between the Nationwide Conference and Division Three now so blurred that it doesn't really matter so much as it did back in 1987 – Scarborough are now not so much non-League as Nationwide Conference League, or on the fifth rung of the national pyramid, call it what you will.

It must be stressed that this book is not a history of Scarborough FC – a comprehensive official history has been written by Steve Adamson – but a collection of interesting images, arranged in roughly chronological order. I therefore make no apologies for people involved with the club down the years who have failed to get a mention. It would be impossible to include them all.

Collecting the images for Scarborough FC was no easy task. An appeal for material in the local press, match programme and on the club's official website produced a very limited response and I came to the conclusion that images prior to the 1970s are simply very thin on the ground.

There are undoubtedly photographs out there that I have not seen but would have loved to have had the chance to include. For example, I have included pictures from away games wherever possible and I am sure there are many more, particularly from the Football League years. To root them out, however, would have been an expensive full-time job, taking many months.

The biggest section of the book covers Scarborough's Football League seasons, from 1987 to 1999. As arguably the most important era in the history of the club to date, this needed an extensive permanent photographic record.

Indeed, an entire book could have been devoted to the Football League years alone, but I wanted to make this a book that spanned all eras and that could appeal to all fans. The division of chapters basically chose itself: the early years up to the Second World War; post-war entry into the Midland League and onto the Northern Premier League; the glorious 1970s, a period probably when, with four Wembley finals and numerous FA Cup runs, that more people in the town watched at least one game a season than at any other time; progress into the Alliance Premier League; the Football League years and, finally, return to the Nationwide Conference and fresh hope for the future. Up the Boro!

Paul Eade
August 2002

One

The Early Years

1879-1939

Possibly the earliest existing photograph relating to Scarborough Football Club. Cabbies watch a game at the recently-opened Athletic Ground from their horse-drawn vehicles in 1898. Some houses on Seamer Road can just be made out on the far right of the picture.

A match in progress at the Athletic Ground in around 1900. The gas cylinder that dominated the view behind the ground, until its dismantlement a few years ago, can be seen in the background.

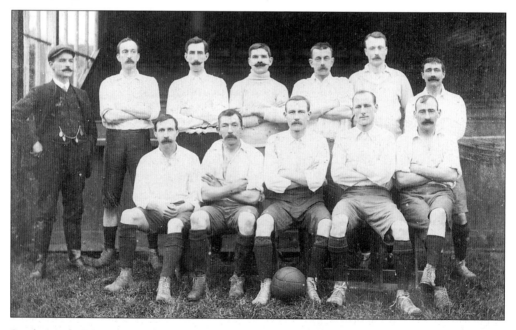

Scarborough FC Former Players XI, 1909. The team played a Scarborough Present FC on 25 December 1909 to raise money for former player Lionel Charlwood, who had become seriously ill. From left to right, back row: Blades, Burrell, Riby, Pollard, Duke, Webster, Hawkins. Front row: Rose, Bartliff, Todd, Nellis, Wharton.

The 1910/11 season team and officials that finished runners-up in the Yorkshire Combination. From left to right, back row: Spavin, Adamson, Cole (chairman), Milnes, Renwick, Brammall, Lin (secretary), Webster (trainer). Middle row: Scott, Allan, Emmerson. Front row: Horsman, F. Johnson, O. Johnson, Blades, Bruce.

Captain Harold Blanckley leads his side out for the match against York City Reserves on 25 September 1926. The Yorkshire League match, in Boro's first season as a professional outfit, ended 0-0 in front of an estimated crowd of 3,500.

Prolific scorer and skipper Billy Clayson holds the Midland League Championship Shield won by Scarborough in 1929/30. Boro won the League by six points in a marathon 50 game season,

amassing 143 goals. They scored five or more goals on no less than eight occasions, including an 11-1 thrashing of Staveley Town in the last home game of the season.

Boro stalwart Les Heelbeck (right) battles for the ball in the FA Cup first round replay at Southport on 29 November 1938. Scarborough held the Third Division side to a 0-0 draw at the Athletic Ground in front of 6,816 spectators, but went down 3-5 in the replay.

The Scarborough side that won the North Riding Senior Cup and Hospital Shield in 1938/39, beating a Middlesbrough XI 3-2 in the latter competition. Players, from left to right, back row: Clarke, Mitchell, Robinson, Rivers, Fieldsend. Middle row: Lister, Meads, Llewellyn, Beckett. Front row: Warwick, Heelbeck, Agar, Jolly. On ground: Paddy and George Waterhouse.

14

Two

Post-War Progress
1945-1972

Scarborough FC, 1945/46. Picking up the pieces after the Second World War, Boro entered the Scarborough & District League, which they won easily, racking up double figure scores in four matches. From left to right, back row: G.E. Giles (director), D. Nichol, W. Kelly, E. Lester, E. Garton, K. Keene, L. Heelbeck (trainer). Front row: G. Dickson, R. Webb, R. Hanson, R. Waterhouse, W. Parke, J. Troy, G. Hartley.

Les Heelbeck. Pictured here sometime in the 1960s, Heelbeck was a member of the 1929/30 Midland League championship side before going on to play for Carlisle, Wolves and Rotherham. He returned to Boro as captain for two seasons before the war and became the club's trainer-coach in 1945.

Colin Appleton. Having made his debut for Boro in 1952 at the age of sixteen, Appleton went on to become one of the club's most successful products. He signed for Leicester City in March 1954 and went on to play in two FA Cup Finals.

Terry Dyson. Malton-born Dyson made his debut for Boro in 1953/54 and went onto play for Tottenham. Pictured here in action for Spurs, Dyson scored the winner in the 1961 FA Cup Final against Leicester, with Colin Appleton on the losing side. He also scored twice in Tottenham's 5-2 victory against Atletico Madrid in the 1963 European Cup Winners' Cup Final.

Reg Halton. Halton was appointed as player-manager at Boro in February 1953, having come to the town as a professional for Scarborough Cricket Club. Seen here leading out his side at the Athletic Ground, Halton played for Manchester United before the war. With Boro struggling in the Midland League, Halton quit after just under a year at the club to join Goole Town.

Scarborough's side pictured at Nottingham Forest on 3 December 1955, where they gained a creditable 1-1 draw against Forest Reserves. From left to right, back row: Lockwood, Matthews, Slatter, Lee, MacKenzie, Myers. Front row: Mitchell, Wood, Parkinson, French, Ware.

Scarborough found things tough in the Midland League for most of the 1950s. Here is a side from 1956/57, when Boro finished second bottom. From left to right, back row: Jim Wilde (trainer), Greenwood, Slatter, -?-, Lee, MacKenzie, Myers, Lockwood. Front row: Bowman, French, Parkinson, Linaker, Ware.

Scarborough lost 6-1 at Kings Lynn on 9 February 1957, one of several heavy defeats during the season. It looks as if the ball is once again heading into the Boro net.

The Athletic Ground photographed around 1960. The now demolished gasworks
dominates the skyline and the locomotive shed, also long gone, can be seen with the

circular ventilator in the roof at the far left of the picture.

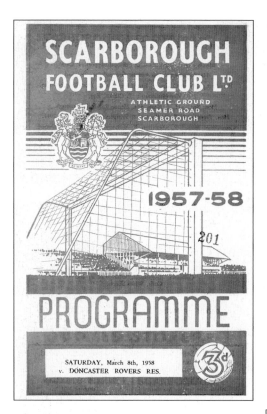

Scarborough's match programme for the visit of Doncaster Rovers Reserves dated 8 March 1958. The game scheduled for that date was in fact postponed and rearranged for the weekend of 4 April, when Boro played two home games in two days, beating Rovers 2-1 on the Friday and Goole 2-0 the following day.

Scarborough played a selected XI on 30 April 1962 as a joint testimonial for Geoff Bowman and Colin Smailes. Both players served Boro well through several difficult seasons in the 1950s, Bowman making 186 first team appearances and Smailes 47.

Mascot Barrie Watson leads out Owen Laffey for a game at the Athletic Ground in the 1962/63 season. Former Sheffield Wednesday defender Laffey was a key figure as Boro's fortunes soared under new player-manager Eddy Brown. Laffey made a total of 365 appearances in a Boro shirt.

Scarborough's team pictured on 15 May 1963. Boro thrashed Stockton to secure the North Eastern League title in a season when they also won the North Eastern League Cup and took Crewe Alexandra to a replay in the FA Cup first round. From left to right, back row: Eddy Brown (manager), Tommy McQuaid, Bill Mordue, Terry Wood, John McCusker, Derek Boyes, Owen Laffey, Alec Betton (trainer). Front row: Barry Dunn, Cliff Jones, Peter Whyke, John Powell, Alan Franks, plus mascots Keith and Barrie Watson.

In 1962 Scarborough issued their own Christmas card. Player manager Eddy Brown is the second from the left on the front row.

Between 1952 and 1968 Scarborough fielded a third team, known as the 'A' team, in the Scarborough and District League. This line-up is from 1963. From left to right, back row: Barnes (director), Bourne (trainer), Rowntree, Soulsby, -?-, Langley, Walker, Widdowfield, Wardell (manager). Front row: Evans, Reed, Dowling, Thompson, Welford.

Former Glasgow Rangers midfielder Albert Franks became Scarborough player-manager for 1964/65 following the shock resignation of Eddy Brown. Franks led Boro to fifth place in the Midland League in 1964/65 but was sacked in December 1965 following a run of five successive defeats.

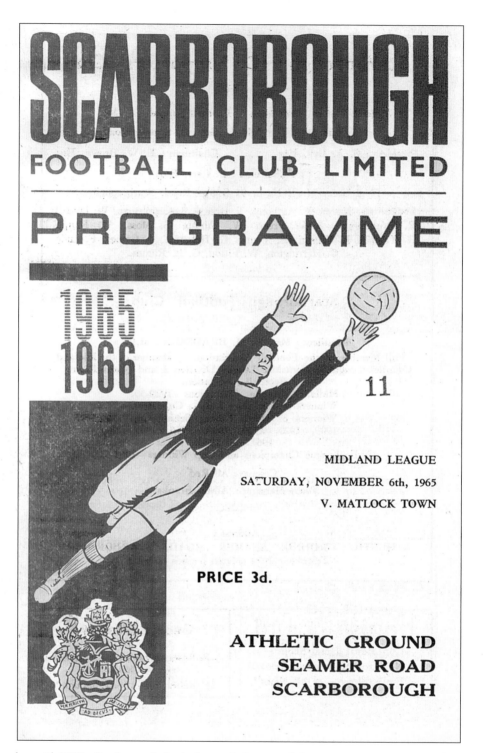

SCARBOROUGH

FOOTBALL CLUB LIMITED

PROGRAMME

1965
1966

11

MIDLAND LEAGUE

SATURDAY, NOVEMBER 6th, 1965

V. MATLOCK TOWN

PRICE 3d.

ATHLETIC GROUND
SEAMER ROAD
SCARBOROUGH

By the mid-1960s Scarborough had changed the matchday programme cover to this very attractive design. Its clear, simple presentation puts to the shame the cluttered covers that so many clubs favour these days.

In 1966/67 Scarborough finished a creditable sixth in the Midland League. From left to right, back row: Bob Entwistle, John McMurran, Terry Wood, Jim Rollo, Ken Boyes, Peter Flynn. Front row: Geoff Bowman, Johny Hamilton, Harry Dunn, Keith Watson (mascot), Jimmy Weir, Bill Marshall, Alan Franks.

Between July 1966 and March 1968 the Boro board of directors took charge of team affairs by committee. From left to right, back row: Bob Whelpton, Derek Watson, John Barnes, David Jenkinson, Bas Good, Les Rollett. Front row: Les Skelton, Tom Stephenson (chairman), Herbert Temple (secretary).

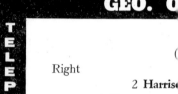

Centre pages from the match programme against Grantham on 20 April 1968. Boro clearly had

no shortage of programme advertisers – but how many of these companies still exist today?

Scarborough finished seventh in the Midland League in 1967/68, when they drew just four of their 40 matches. From left to right, back row: Carr, Laffey, Dunn, Flynn, Rollo, Davey, McMurran, Bowman. Front row: Murray, McMillan, Adamson, Franks, Waring, Keith Watson (mascot).

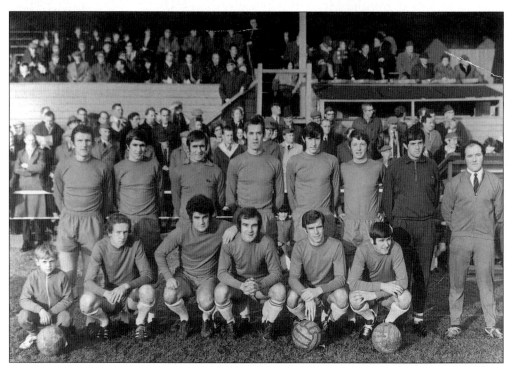

Colin Appleton returned to Scarborough as player-manager in the summer of 1969. He is on the far left of the back row in this line-up for the start of the 1969/70 campaign.

A mixture of first-team players, fringe players and trialists would suggest that this 1970/71 line up was for a reserve game. From left to right, back row: Wardell (trainer), Thundercliffe, Williams, Dawson, Burden, -?-, Appleton. Front row: Driver, Barmby, Franks, Davis, -?-.

Harry Dunn collects the Player of the Year award for 1970 from Charles Sharp, general manager of Scarborough and District Newspapers. The reliable defender amassed over 900 appearances in a Boro shirt in a career spanning the period 1964 to 1983.

Programme for the friendly against Huddersfield Town for the official opening of the floodlight system on 26 October 1970. The lights were actually used for the first time on 16 September 1970, when Boro beat Boston United 2-1.

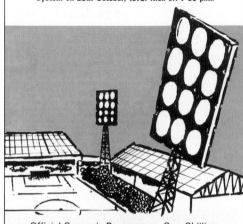

Boro put together a 17-match unbeaten run in the Northern Premier League in 1971/72, when they finished fourth. The last match in that sequence was a 1-1 draw at home to Fleetwood on 1 January 1972, when Boro lined up as, from left to right, back row: Geoff Bowman (trainer), Storey, Thompson, Siddle, Shoulder, Appleton (player-manager), Potter (substitute). Front row: Dunn, Fagan, Smethurst, Barmby, Lee, Dale.

Three

The Glorious Seventies
1972-1979

Scarborough players, staff and officials, including chairman Don Robinson (back row, second from right), celebrate the club's third FA Trophy Final success within the space of five years after beating Dagenham 2-1 at Wembley on 14 May 1977. This era saw Scarborough become one of the country's leading non-League sides and the foundations were laid to stake a claim for a place in the Football League.

Photograph by Ray Mantell, Grosvenor Studio, Scarborough

Wednesday, October 18th, 1972.

3P

SCARBOROUGH
v
BRADFORD P.A.

NORTHERN PREMIER LEAGUE

By 1972/73 Scarborough had adopted a photographic cover for its matchday programme. Consistent form throughout the season saw Boro finish runners-up to Boston United in the Northern Premier League.

Scarborough (left) and Wigan Athletic take to the field at Wembley for the 1973 FA Trophy Final. A contingent of Boro fans in the 23,000 crowd can be seen in the background.

Malcolm Leask (partly hidden, on ground) puts Boro 1-0 ahead against Wigan in the twelfth minute. Signed from South Shields at the start of the 1972/73 season, Leask proved a prolific scorer, netting 41 times in 118 appearances for Scarborough.

Malcolm Thompson (number 10) established an effective partnership up front with Malcolm Leask for both the 1972/73 and 1973/74 campaigns. Here he wins the ball against Wigan, against whom he scored the extra-time winner in Boro's 2-1 Wembley success.

Malcolm Leask (number 9) once again causes problems for the Wigan defence at Wembley, with Malcolm Thompson running forward in anticipation.

Player-manager Colin Appleton (number 2) urges his players to give one last effort before extra-time against Wigan. Having been on the losing side in two FA Cup finals as a player with Leicester, Appleton was determined to make this Wembley appearance third time lucky.

We've done it! Exhausted, rain-soaked but jubilant Boro players hold aloft the FA Trophy in front of Wembley's Royal Box after the 2-1 defeat of Wigan Athletic.

Just two days after beating Wigan Athletic, Boro were back in action at the Athletic Ground, beating Billingham Synthonia 4-1 in the North Riding Senior Cup final. A superb season, in which Boro played no less than 75 competitive fixtures, also saw the club win the Vaux Floodlit League and reach the second round of the FA Cup.

The 1973/74 season saw the departure of Colin Appleton to Grimsby on 3 November. Subsequently coached by Gerry Donoghue and Ken Boyes, both in caretaker roles, Boro finished fifth in the Northern Premier League. From left to right, back row: Wardell (trainer), Lee, Fountain, Thompson, Garrow, Leask, Dodds, Dunn, Appleton (manager). Front row: Todd, Franks, Donoghue, Fagan, Hewitt.

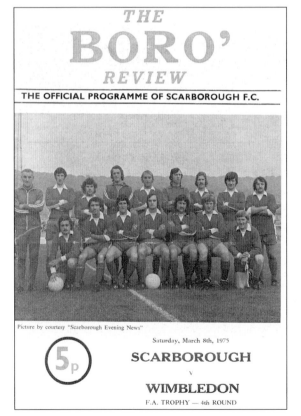

THE

BORO'

REVIEW

THE OFFICIAL PROGRAMME OF SCARBOROUGH F.C.

Picture by courtesy "Scarborough Evening News"

5p

Saturday, March 8th, 1975

SCARBOROUGH

v

WIMBLEDON

F.A. TROPHY — 4th ROUND

Scarborough embarked on another FA Trophy run in 1974/75 under the management of Ken Houghton. On 8 March 1975, 8,105 spectators crammed into the Athletic Ground to see Boro beat Wimbledon 1-0 with a goal from Tony Aveyard.

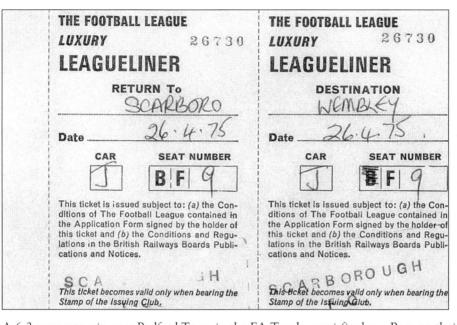

A 6-2 aggregate win over Bedford Town in the FA Trophy semi-final saw Boro on their way to Wembley once more, this time to face Matlock Town. Among the fleet of trains making its way to Wembley from Scarborough was the Football League Luxury Leagueliner, a special supporters' train complete with disco.

Boro players in buoyant mood at Wembley ahead of the 1975 FA Trophy final. From left to right, back row: Wardell (trainer), Pettit, Fountain, Aveyard, Marshall, Dunn, Houghton, Williams, Don Robinson (chairman), Davidson. Front row: Barmby, Woodall, Connolly, Glenn Houghton (mascot), Todd, Hewitt, Dale.

Scarborough players acknowledge their supporters as they emerge at Wembley for the FA Trophy final against Matlock. Scarborough lost the game 4-0 despite enjoying the majority of possession in the game.

Despite the 4-0 defeat by Matlock, Boro received a great reception from their fans on their return to Scarborough. Chairman Don Robinson is holding the FA Trophy runners-up shield.

Full-back Charlie Fountain was a club stalwart during Boro's Wembley glory years, notching a total of 230 appearances for Boro. However, he never started a Trophy Final, only figuring as a substitute in the 1975 defeat by Matlock Town.

In May 1975 Scarborough made a brief tour of Gibraltar, playing two competitive fixtures. Pictured in front of the Rock are, from left to right, back row: Wardell (trainer), Marshall,

Dunn, Williams, Woodall, Hewitt, Davidson, Connelly. Front row: Todd, Barmby, Pettit, Fountain, Houghton (manager), Dale.

In 1975/76, with Colin Appleton back in the manager's seat, Scarborough enjoyed another memorable season, including reaching the third round of the FA Cup, where they lost 2-1 at home to Crystal Palace. The second round saw Boro put Third Division Preston North End to the sword with a 3-2 victory in front of a 4,100 crowd at the Athletic Ground.

A narrow 1-0 victory over two legs against Enfield in the FA Trophy semi-final saw Boro back at Wembley on 24 April to face fellow Northern Premier League side Stafford Rangers.

Defender Sean Marshall (number 3) looks on as Scarborough repel a Stafford raid in the 1976 FA Trophy Final. Stafford twice took the lead only for Boro to level the scores with goals from John Woodall and Derek Abbey.

Two minutes from the end of extra time Scarborough were awarded a penalty following a handball and Sean Marshall confidently converted the spot-kick to give Scarborough a 3-2 victory over Stafford. Note that Boro players Billy Ayre and Harry A. Dunn have their backs turned away from the goal even though the ball isn't yet in the net.

Scarborough captain Harry Dunn collects the FA Trophy in 1976. Dunn played in all four of Boro's Wembley finals.

Derek Abbey, scorer of Scarborough's second goal against Stafford, (left, with cap), is among this group of Boro players acknowledging the fans in a lap of honour at Wembley.

In May 1977 Scarborough were back at Wembley again. A group of fans in the Boro shop show off a ticket for the FA Trophy Final against Dagenham.

Ticket for the 1977 FA Trophy Final. To get there, Boro had to play 12 ties, including replays against Walthamstow Avenue and Hitchin Town, an abandoned game against Nuneaton Borough followed by another replay and two replays against Altrincham after their two-legged semi-final finished 2-2 on aggregate. Due to their fixture backlog, Boro played eight Northern Premier League matches in May and their season did not end until 20 May.

Scarborough boss Colin Appleton leads out his side against Dagenham for the FA Trophy final at Wembley on 14 May 1977. The electronic scoreboard is advertising the England *v*. Wales home international to be played at Wembley at the end of the same month.

Dagenham held a 1-0 lead for much of the 1977 FA Trophy Final but sustained Boro pressure finally paid off in the 86th minute. A handball was awarded against Dagenham as Derek Abbey tried to score and Harry A. Dunn equalised from the penalty spot.

With extra time looming, Derek Abbey was on hand to score in a Wembley final for the second successive year, after Jeff Barmby (left) set him up.

Scarborough celebrate at Wembley for the third time following the 2-1 victory over Dagenham. Tragically, Tony Aveyard (far right), died just a few days later after sustaining a serious head injury in a Northern Premier League match against Boston United. A speedy winger, twenty-one-year-old Aveyard had trials with Middlesbrough, Manchester United, Arsenal and Burnley and his death stunned the whole town.

Scarborough captain Harry Dunn (right) and Sean Marshall come onto the pitch at the

Athletic Ground with the FA Trophy the club retained in 1977.

Boro competed in an Anglo-Italian tournament in 1976 and 1977. Highlights included a 4-0 trouncing of Udinese in 1976 and a 1-0 victory over Parma the following year.

Scarborough officials Bob Whelpton (centre left) and Derek Watson (centre right) welcome two Italian club representatives at Manchester Airport, probably in 1977.

Scarborough show off their trophy collection at the start of the 1977/78 season. From left to right, back row: Harris, Marshall, Fountain, Chapman, Abbey, H. Dunn, Blampey. Front row: R. Smith, Donoghue, Woodall, H.A. Dunn, D. Smith. Trophies won the previous season are, left to right: Yorkshire Television Award, Greenalls Northern Premier League Cup, FA Trophy, North Riding Senior Cup.

Harry A. Dunn. When Harry Dunn joined Boro in 1975, Scarborough had two players called Harry Dunn on their books. To differentiate him, the new arrival acquired a fictitious 'A' initial. Harry A. Dunn represented Scarborough 265 times, scoring 65 goals.

As well as their FA Trophy successes, Scarborough acquired a reputation for FA Cup runs in the 1970s. In 1978/79 they won 1-0 at Chorley in the first round proper before losing 3-0 at York City in the second round.

The 1978/79 season was Scarborough's last in the Northern Premier League, their placing of fourth comfortably securing a place in the new national Alliance Premier League for the next season. From left to right, back row: Fountain, Gauden, H. Dunn, Maltby, McKechnie, Abbey, Marshall, Ellis, H.A. Dunn. Front row: Harris, Lyall, Donoghue, Dennis, R. Smith.

Four

Into a National Division

Ray McHale congratulates Stuart Mell after the latter scored against Weymouth in Scarborough's last game of the 1986/87 season. By then, Boro had already secured promotion to the Football League.

Christmas card issued by the club in 1979, Scarborough's first season in the newly formed Alliance Premier League. The banner on the right reads 'Wembley? 1980' but ironically Boro went out of the FA Trophy in the first round. The American footballers are explained in the picture below.

Roberto D'Oliveria (left) and Ivan Belfiore (right), with chairman Don Robinson. Both players came to the club on loan from American side Detroit Express. Belfiore played four first team games at left-back and impressed manager Colin Appleton.

Midfielder Pat Olney (right), seen here in action in October 1980. Olney spent over five seasons at the Athletic Ground, scoring some important goals.

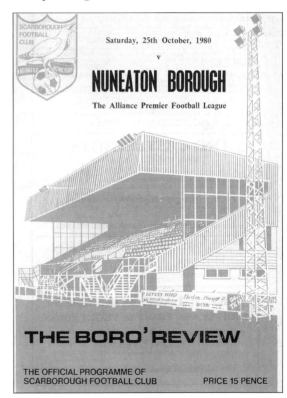

Scarborough won their first seven home games in 1980/81, including a 2-1 victory over Nuneaton Borough on 25 October. Their good start, and a strong finish to the season ensured that Boro finished third in the Alliance Premier League.

Richard Dixey (centre), wins a header in a match at the Athletic Ground in January 1981. Dixey was signed from Nuneaton Borough early in the 1979/80 season and proved very reliable at the heart of the Scarborough defence.

Former Rotherham manager Jimmy McAnearney took over as Scarborough boss in January 1981, following the resignation of Colin Appleton. Scarborough finished a respectable seventh in the Alliance Premier League in 1981/82, but McAnearney left shortly before the end of the season.

The Athletic Ground looking towards the Edgehill Road end in June 1981. The covered accommodation at the far end was destroyed by rampaging Wolves hooligans in August 1987.

Colin Williams (number 10) scores the penalty that earned Scarborough a 1-1 draw against Boston United on 9 September 1981. Williams was ever-present in his only season at Boro and cracked in 33 goals in 51 appearances, making him the Alliance Premier League's top scorer.

On 3 May 1982, a testimonial for former manager Colin Appleton (left), saw a team of present Boro players beat a past Boro side 5-2. Lining up with Appleton are (from left), Gerry Donoghue, Jeff Barmby and Harry Dunn. The four players pictured amassed over 1,900 appearances for Scarborough between them.

Former Bradford City forward John Hanson was one of several players brought in by new manager John Cottom for the 1982/83 season . Here Hanson scores one of his brace in the FA Cup first round tie at Tranmere Rovers, where Boro went down 4-2.

Scarborough Reserves won the Northern Counties East Division One (North) in 1982/83, with 17 wins from 26 matches. From left to right, back row: G. Bowman, J. Bowman, Abbey, Cook, Robinson, Gosling, Fountain, Gretton, John Taylor (coach). Front row: Pickard, Brown, D. Bowman, Hartley, Exley, Alderslade, Dickens.

Malcolm Smith celebrates a Scarborough goal in the 3-1 victory at Stalybridge Celtic in the FA Trophy second round tie on 5 February 1983.

Boro's reward for winning at Stalybridge was a trip to Telford. Although Dick Dawson managed to get a shot in here, the hosts, who had a very formidable home record, ran out 3-0 winners.

Supporters gather for the trip to Marine for an FA Trophy first round tie on 14 January 1984.
The fans may not have looked so happy on the way home – Scarborough lost 2-1.

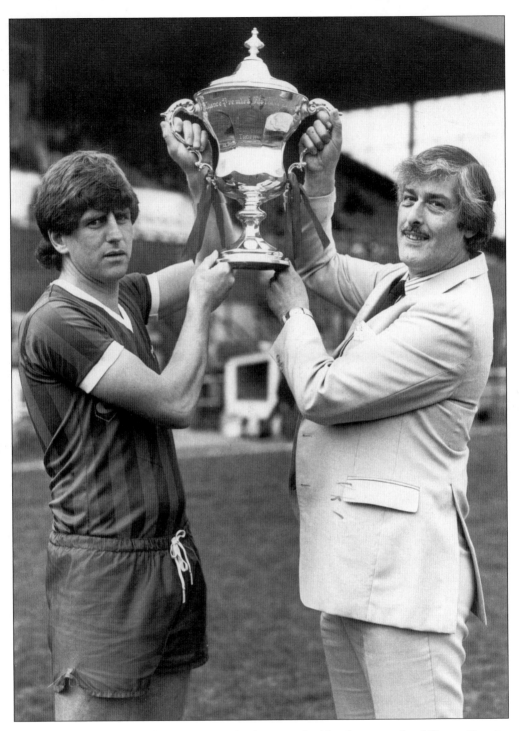

Early exits in the FA Trophy, FA Cup and a lower mid-table placing in the Alliance Premier League in 1983/84 were compensated for with success in the Bob Lord Trophy. Scarborough beat Barnet 2-1 on aggregate in the two-legged final. Player manager John Cottom and chairman Tony Burnard display the Trophy at the Athletic Ground.

The 1984/85 season saw Scarborough finish a respectable sixth in the now named Gola League. Striker Trenton Wiggan launches a shot on goal during Boro's 5-0 demolition of Dagenham on 6 October.

Scarborough suffered FA Cup disappointment for the second season running when they went out in the fourth qualifying round, beaten 1-0 at Northern League side Tow Law. Dave Bowman battles for possession in a match that turned out to be John Cottom's last as Boro manager.

With Harry Dunn back at Boro in the manager's chair, the club made a bright start to the 1985/86 season. Gary Hooley converts a penalty, one of two goals by the striker that gave Scarborough a 2-1 victory over Nuneaton Borough on 26 August.

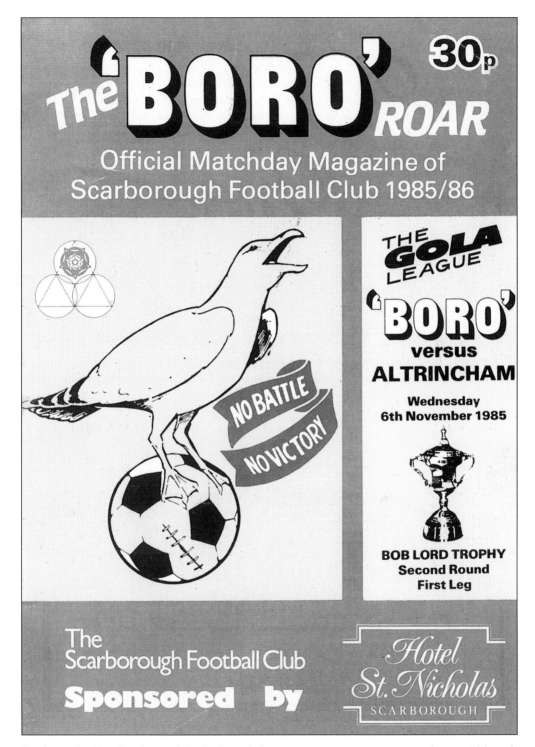

By the mid-1980s Scarborough had adopted this attractive programme cover design. Although Scarborough won this Bob Lord second round, first leg tie against Altrincham 3-2, their opponents overturned the deficit in the return match with a 2-0 success.

Scarborough had to start the 1985/86 FA Cup competition from the first qualifying round. They made it to the first round with a 4-1 defeat of Bishop Auckland in the fourth qualifying round when Marshall Burke (centre), was one of the scorers. Boro lost 6-1 at Notts County in the first round proper.

Barry Adamson, a long-serving director, became Scarborough chairman in March 1986. Tragically, he collapsed and died at the age of just forty-seven while attempting to break up fighting on the terraces in Boro's FA Trophy tie against Morecambe on 20 December 1986.

Neil Warnock took over as Scarborough boss in the summer of 1986. His side were completely unfancied to win the league, now named the GM Vauxhall Conference, in 1986/87. However, a 22 match unbeaten run commenced at the start of November. By the New Year, Boro were firmly in contention for the championship and grabbed another three points with a 1-0 win at Enfield on 10 January. Ray McHale (centre), looks on as Enfield raid the Boro goal.

A 1-0 win at Kidderminster on 18 April, put Scarborough firmly in the driving seat over nearest rivals Barnet. Stuart Mell attempts a shot in the game at Aggborough.

Monday, 20th April, 1987

Scarborough Football Club

welcomes

Runcorn

GM Vauxhall Conference

Scarborough Football Club

Members of the
GM/Vauxhall Conference League 1986/87

MAJOR SPONSOR—SCARBOROUGH BUILDING SOCIETY

*The BORO celebrates
its Diamond Jubilee Year as a Professional Club 1926 — 1986*

Today's Match Ball Sponsor is:-
THE EDWARD HARLAND
SCARBOROUGH & DISTRICT
FOOTBALL LEAGUE

30p

Championship fever was in the air when Runcorn visited the Athletic Ground on 20 April. Victory would have almost wrapped up the title but, in front of 3,764 spectators, Boro's unbeaten run came to a shock end with a 2-1 defeat to keep fans biting their fingernails.

A 2-0 win at Sutton United on 25 April put Scarborough within touching distance of the title. Local-born player Mitch Cook (right), slammed in Boro's second.

Mitch Cook turns away to celebrate at Sutton, with Stuart Mell in pursuit and jubilant Boro fans in the background.

Ray McHale and Scarborough fans mob Mitch Cook after his goal against Sutton United. Four days

later Barnet lost 2-1 to Stafford Rangers, handing Scarborough the GM Vauxhall Conference title.

Scarborough captain Cec Podd holds the GM Vauxhall Conference Championship Trophy aloft after Scarborough's 2-1 victory over Weymouth on 2 May 1987. The championship meant that Scarborough became the first club ever to gain automatic promotion to the Football League.

Five

Football League
Ups and Downs

Scarborough players celebrate after beating Chelsea 4-3 on aggregate in the Littlewoods Cup on 4 October 1989. From left to right, back row: Paul Olsson, Steve Norris, Mick Clarke. Front row: Steve Saunders, Gary Brook, Alan Kamara, Tommy Graham, Paul Robinson.

As a club currently marking occupation of the same ground for League football for half a century, Leyton Orient this afternoon take pride in playing host to the competition's newcomers Scarborough for their first away fixture.

Scarborough Football Club was formed on an amateur basis in 1879 and turned professional in the 1920s.

Members of many leagues during their history, they were founders of the Alliance Premier League — nowadays the GM Vauxhall Conference — in 1979.

The Boro' were Midland League champions in 1930 and North Eastern League winners in 1963, taking the League Cup the same season. They have won the North Riding Senior Cup on 16 occasions and the Yorkshire League Cup once.

Their most successful period in cup football was during the 1970s. Then the Boro' reached four FA Trophy Finals at Wembley in five years and emerged winners of their meetings with Wigan Athletic, Stafford Rangers and Dagenham.

Manager during this period was Scarborough-born Colin Appleton who, after a long and distinguished playing career in the League, mainly with Leicester City, returned to manage his home-town club and steer them to unprecedented cup success.

The club's greatest achievement, of course, came last season when they won the GM Vauxhall Conference to become the first to earn automatic promotion to the Football League.

We wish them a long and successful association.

KEVIN BLACKWELL (Goalkeeper) Signed in October, 1986 from Barnet who, ironically, challenged Boro' throughout last season for the GM Vauxhall championship. His arrival coincided with the start of the club's 22-match unbeaten run. Named Player of the Year. Lives in Luton and makes a 450 mile round trip to home games.

LES McJANNETT (Defender) Close season from Matlock Town previously with Mansfield. A tion to the club's Scottish contingent.

NEIL THOMPSON (Defender) A survivor pre-Neil Warnock era, he joined Boro' from H Had made 181 appearances scoring 22 times the club gained the Football League memb Earned four England semi-professional caps la son and was the club's only ever-present.

IAN BENNYWORTH (Defender) Joined Bc summer from Nuneaton Borough after experien Hull City. Played 49 games last season and scor goals.

STEVE RICHARDS (Defender) 25. Made than 100 League appearances for Hull with wt was apprenticed York, Lincoln and Cambridge tive of Dundee, he played 40 games last seas scored twice.

PAUL KENDALL (Defender) Joined the s club in the summer of 1986 from home town Town for whom he had played 106 League game sed just two of the Boro's 52 matches last seaso

STEWART HAMILL (Midfield) Signed from cham towards the end of last season and made n pearances, scoring twice. A Glaswegian previous Leicester and Northampton.

RAY McHALE (Midfield) 37. Much travelled who has assisted Chesterfield, Halifax, Sw Brighton, Barnsley, Sheffield United, Bury, Sw and Rochdale. Signed for Boro' last season and 23 appearances, scoring two goals.

ERNIE MOSS (Forward) 37. Signed from Stc in July for a £4,000 fee. Vastly experienced, t made almost 700 League appearances with Ct field, Peterborough, Mansfield, Port Vale, Lincoln caster and Stockport. When the season star needed 11 more goals to join the elite band wh scored 250 times in Football League matches.

STEWART MELL (Forward) 29. Born Don Came to Boro' from Burton Albion after previous ence with Appleby Frodingham, Doncaster and H Has been capped by England at semi-profe. level. Club's leading scorer last season with 18 g 46 matches.

PHIL WALKER (Forward) 30. Born Kirkby. S in 1986 after experience with Chesterfield, Roth and Mansfield. Scored 15 times in 41 appearar 1986/87.

CEC PODD (Defender) 35. Born St. Kitts experienced full-back who made over 500 appea for Bradford and Halifax before joining Scarborc the summer of 1986. Club skipper who made 43 a ances last season.

ANDY HARRISON (Midfield) Played 17 tim season after joining the club the previous summe viously with Burton, Boston United and Ketterin also played abroad with Christchurch, New Ze and Hellenic, South Africa.

DAVE BOWMAN (Forward) Scarborough bc son of the club's trainer. Has made 146 appearan the club, scoring 50 goals, but missed virtually the of last season with a severe back injury from wf has now happily recovered.

SCARBOROUGH
Athletic Ground, Scarborough

Manager: Neil Warnock

Achievements:
FA Trophy Winners 1973, 1976, 1977
Runners-up 1975
GM Vauxhall Conference Champions
1987

Additional honours:
Bob Lord Trophy winners, Northern Premier League runners-up, Northern Premier League Cup winners, Twice Vaux Floodlight League winners, Yorkshire League Cup winners, North Eastern League and Cup winners, Midland League winners, North Riding Senior Cup winners (on 16 occasions).
Record home attendance: 11, 124 v Luton Town, 1938.

After drawing 2-2 at home to Wolves in their first Football League game on 15 August 1987, Scarborough travelled to Brisbane Road to face Leyton Orient on 22

SCARBOROUGH

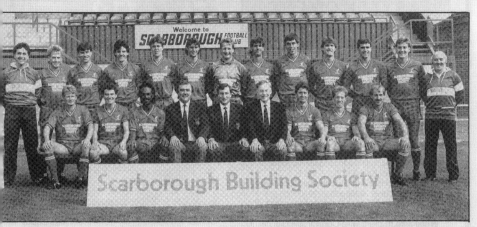

ick row (left to right): Paul Evans (assistant manager), Steve Adams, Tommy Graham, Andy Harrison, Phil
er, Ian Bennyworth, Kevin Blackwell, Steve Richards, Ernie Moss, Paul Kendall, Neil Thompson, Mitch
k and Geoff Bowman (trainer).
ont row: Les McJannet, David Bowman, Ces Podd, T. Wood (chairman), Neil Warnock (manager), John
cett (vice chairman), Stewart Mell, Stewart Hamill, Ray McHale.
hoto: Scarborough and District Newspapers).

August. This is the centre spread of the matchday programme from the game that
Boro lost 3-1.

Midfielder Ray McHale joined Scarborough from Swansea City in December 1986 and made a significant contribution to Boro's Conference championship winning run. He then scored the equaliser that earnt Boro a 2-2 draw in their first Football League match against Wolves.

Scarborough made a very satisfactory start to life in the Fourth Division, finishing in twelfth position. Experienced midfielder Tommy Graham (right), missed just one competitive match during the season. Here he celebrates a Boro goal with Stewart Hammill (left) and Doug Newton (centre).

Local-born players became something of a rarity for Scarborough in the Football League. One exception was Tony Outhart, who scored in Boro's biggest away win of 1987/88, a 4-0 victory at Newport County on 12 April.

Scarborough ended their first Football League season with a 1-1 draw at home to Stockport County on 9 May 1988. Boro's Steve Adams (right), battles for possession with Stockport captain, Bill Williams.

Manager Neil Warnock brought in new faces for a promotion bid in the 1988/89 season. Striker Steve Norris (top), was signed for £50,000 from Telford United, with Colin Morris (front), drafted in as player-coach.

Scarborough began their 1988/89 campaign with a 0-0 draw against Tranmere Rovers on 27 August. This stylish programme cover design was introduced for the new season.

Forward Gary Brook (right), was a £10,000 signing from Newport County. He is seen challenging Tranmere 'keeper Eric Nixon in Boro's 1988/89 curtain-raiser.

By November, it was clear that manager Neil Warnock had put together a side capable of winning promotion. His team were unbeaten at the now re-named McCain Stadium and knocked Second Division Portsmouth out of the Littlewoods Cup.

Steve Norris and Gary Brook formed a good strike partnership for Boro in 1988/89. Here Norris' shot is about to strike the crossbar in the 0-0 draw with Leyton Orient on 8 October.

Bye bye. Little did fans know that Neil Warnock was managing Scarborough for the last time in the 2-1 win over Crewe Alexandra on 31 December 1988. With Boro lying third in the Fourth Division, Warnock resigned in acrimonious circumstances, blaming boardroom interference. His departure effectively marked the end of Boro's golden era in the Football League, in terms of success and stability.

Colin Morris stepped into the manager's chair after Neil Warnock's departure but Boro's form stuttered in the New Year. Fans look on in the 2-0 defeat by Hereford United on 28 January.

To revive Boro's flagging fortunes, manager Colin Morris made a record £105,000 signing of midfielder Martin Russell from Leicester City in February 1989. Russell proved a class act as Scarborough made the play-offs, and although he scored in the latter it was not enough as Boro lost 2-1 on aggregate against Leyton Orient.

Mick Clarke was signed from Barnsley in the summer of 1989 for £10,000. Here he is in action against a Bermuda XI, who Boro beat 7-0 in a friendly on 7 August.

Scarborough started the 1989/90 season brightly, including a Littlewoods Cup win over Scunthorpe United. Steve Richards (far left), scores the second goal with a header in the 2-0 win in the first round, first leg game on 23 August.

Scarborough's reward for beating
Scunthorpe was a second round tie
against Chelsea in the Littlewoods Cup.
In the first leg at Stamford Bridge on 19
September, a backs-to-the-wall
performance saw Boro earn a 1-1 draw
after taking an early lead through a
Chelsea own goal.

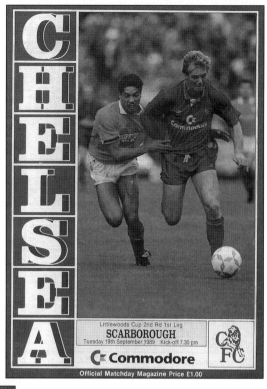

Littlewoods Cup 2nd Rd 1st Leg
SCARBOROUGH
Tuesday 19th September 1989   Kick-off 7.30 pm

C≣ **Commodore**

Official Matchday Magazine Price £1.00

Paul Olsson on the attack for Scarborough
in the return leg against Chelsea at the
McCain Stadium. Boro were 2-0 down with
20 minutes to go but Tommy Graham and
teenager Paul Robinson levelled the scores.

Hot on the heels of the equaliser, Scarborough were awarded a penalty. Martin Russell calmly sent Chelsea 'keeper Dave Beasant the wrong way with his spot kick as Scarborough completed

a sensational 3-2 win over the London giants in one of the most memorable nights in the club's history.

Former manager Colin Appleton remained a regular visitor to Scarborough in a scouting capacity. Here he was spotted at a Scarborough Reserves match against Wrexham in November 1989.

Alan Kamara (right), launches a challenge in the 2-2 draw against Colchester on 3 February 1990. The defender became a firm favourite with fans in three and a half seasons as a regular in the Boro side.

Colin Morris was sacked as Scarborough manager in November 1989 as the side's league form slid. Ray McHale took over as boss and after a disastrous run of defeats, managed to steer Boro to safety. McHale brought in several experienced players including former Burnley striker George Oghani, pictured on his first day of training with the club.

Steve Richards in pre-season training under the watchful eye of Ray McHale. By the summer of 1990, Richards, who clocked up 164 appearances at the heart of the defence, was the only surviving player on Boro's books from their Conference winning side.

Red Star Belgrade were the visitors to Scarborough for a pre-season friendly on 30 July 1990. Scarborough scored through Lee Hirst and Adie Meyer but lost 4-2.

Scarborough secured a shirt sponsorship deal from Black Death Vodka for the 1990/91 season. Paul Dobson models the shirt with its 'dripping blood' logo in July 1990.

The left-back berth had been a problem for Scarborough during 1989/90. Manager Ray McHale therefore signed experienced full-back David Logan from Stockport County to fill the position for the start of the 1990/91 campaign.

Scarborough were bizarrely forced to tone down the Black Death Vodka logo at the start of the season, removing the 'dripping blood'. Paul Dobson (right), is wearing the new sanitised version in the first home game of the season against Chesterfield.

How wide do you want the goal? Ray McHale looks anguished in the league match against Doncaster Rovers on 7 October 1990.

McHale had reason to be cheerful by the final whistle against Doncaster. George Oghani (right), turns away after netting Boro's second to secure a 2-1 win.

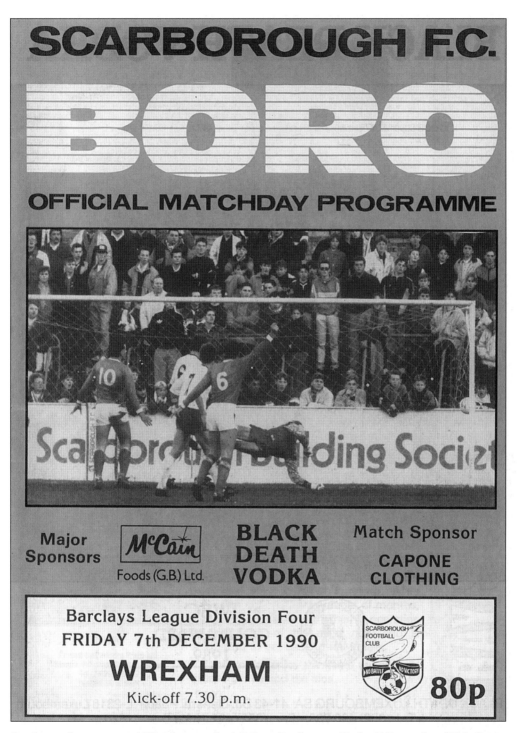

SCARBOROUGH F.C.

BORO

OFFICIAL MATCHDAY PROGRAMME

Major Sponsors *McCain* Foods (G.B.) Ltd.

BLACK DEATH VODKA

Match Sponsor CAPONE CLOTHING

Barclays League Division Four
FRIDAY 7th DECEMBER 1990
WREXHAM
Kick-off 7.30 p.m.

SCARBOROUGH FOOTBALL CLUB

NO BATTLE NO VICTORY

80p

Scarborough entertained Wrexham at the McCain Stadium on Friday 7 December 1990. On an unbelievably wet night, with a howling gale and blizzard, the game was somehow given the go-ahead on a completely waterlogged pitch. Boro won an entertaining game 4-2 – but only 625 spectators turned up to watch.

High hopes were placed on former Glasgow Rangers midfielder John McDonald, signed at the start of the 1989/90 season. But as Boro's form slumped in October and November 1990, McDonald became one of the scapegoats and was axed from the side.

Ray McHale puts goalkeeper Ian Ironside through his paces in a training session on Scarborough's South Bay beach. Ironside proved a very consistent 'keeper and later had a spell with Middlesbrough.

Andrew Fletcher (centre), in action for Scarborough Reserves against local side Eastfield in the winter of 1990/91. Fletcher, signed from Middlesbrough, was one of several younger players the club looked to at the end of the 1990/91 season, in which they finished ninth in Division Four.

Andy Mockler (left) and Tommy Mooney (right) were two more youngsters signed by Ray McHale, from Arsenal and Aston Villa respectively. It soon became clear that Mooney was a shrewd signing, as he quickly showed a keen eye for goal.

Boro players celebrate Lee Hirst's goal in the 2-2 draw against York City on 5 January 1991. Although games against York had been few and far between prior to Scarborough's promotion, they were quickly instated as Boro's local rivals in the Football League.

Following the damage done to the pitch during the Wrexham match, the McCain Stadium was left virtually grassless after snow was cleared away for the game against Hartlepool on 16 February. Lee Hirst ploughs his way through the mud with piles of snow clearly visible in the background.

Striker Darren Foreman was signed from Crewe in March 1991. On his first day of training with his new club, he was still in his former club's kit.

John Ashdjian heads home against Walsall on 31 August 1991. Boro lost the game 3-2 as they began the season shakily, with a very leaky defence.

Adie Meyer wins a header during Scarborough's 2-0 defeat at Gillingham on 7 September 1991. The result left Boro still looking for their first win of the season after five games.

Winger John Reed had a very successful loan spell from Sheffield United in 1990/91 and Ray McHale was able to bring him back for a second spell at the club in September 1991. Reed played seven games but did not make the same impact as he had done first time round.

In a bid to shore up Scarborough's defence, former Northern Ireland international goalkeeper Phil Hughes was signed from Wigan Athletic in October 1991. He lasted until mid-February in a season when six different 'keepers were used.

Steve Carter, a speedy and skilful forward signed from Manchester United, was billed as Boro's big hope when he arrived on the scene midway through the 1990/91 season. In 1991/92 he became seemingly disillusioned and was allowed to leave after just a handful of appearances.

Tommy Mooney, on the other hand, went from strength to strength in 1991/92. Strong, determined and with a powerful shot, he soon became the undisputed star of the team.

On 4 April 1992, Scarborough looked set to settle for a draw against Gillingham until a long-range shot from Mark Jules deceived 'keeper Harvey Lim to give Boro a 2-1 victory. Chris Curran follows up to make certain.

Owen McGee skips through the water during the 2-2 draw against Cardiff City on 14 April. With Boro entrenched in mid-table, only 935 spectators turned up to the game.

Tommy Mooney with the Scarborough Evening News Player of the Season award for 1991/92. Mooney missed just one competitive game during the season and his level of commitment made him very popular among the fans.

Chairman Geoffrey Richmond speaks out at a forum at the club on 19 June 1992. Richmond started a rugby league club, Scarborough Pirates, but they lasted just one season, being forced to fold due to lack of support.

Manager Ray McHale was set a clear target by Geoffrey Richmond for the 1992/93 season. The chairman offered season ticket holders a free pass for the following season unless Scarborough achieved promotion or made the play-offs.

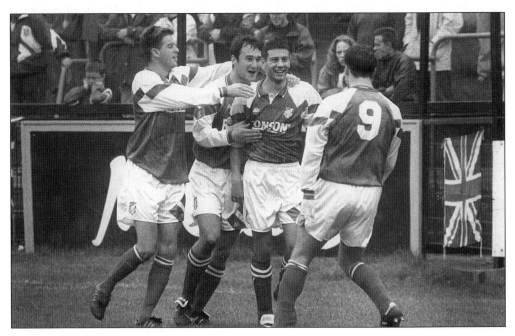

Scarborough started the 1992/93 season very brightly, losing just two of the first 13 league fixtures. John Ashdjian (centre), is congratulated after scoring in the 1-1 draw against Doncaster Rovers on 26 September.

Scarborough resumed their cup giant killing with a remarkable victory over Coventry City in the Coca-Cola Cup second round. Having lost the first leg 2-0 at Highfield Road, Scarborough grabbed the tie with three late goals at the McCain Stadium to run out 3-2 winners on aggregate. The Boro goalscorers celebrate, from left to right: Tommy Mooney, Lee Hirst and Darren Foreman.

Scarborough put Plymouth Argyle to the sword in the Coca-Cola Cup third round. After a 3-3 draw at Plymouth, Scarborough won the replay 2-1. Tommy Mooney heads Boro's first goal past Plymouth goalkeeper, Peter Shilton.

Boro earned a glamour tie against Arsenal in the Coca-Cola Cup fourth round. The game was postponed from 23 December because of a frozen pitch. When it went ahead, on 6 January, the match was a disappointment, being played in thick fog and on a very heavy pitch as Scarborough went down 1-0.

Kyle Lightbourne celebrates his goal in the 3-2 win over Crewe Alexandra on 30 January 1992. The Bermudan international forward was released at the end of the season but went on to play for Walsall, Coventry City, Fulham and Stoke City.

Simon Thompson proved a very reliable full-back for several seasons. Signed from Rotherham United towards the end of the 1991/92 season, he clocked up 136 appearances in a Boro shirt.

Vastly experienced defender Brendan Ormsby was signed from Doncaster Rovers for the 1992/93 season. Formerly of Aston Villa and Leeds United, Ormsby went on to manage Irish side Waterford Town.

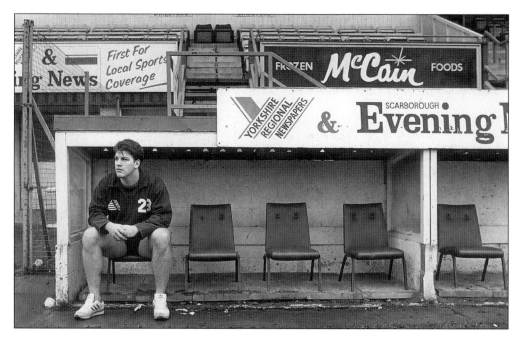

Central defender Adie Meyer sat out the whole of the 1992/93 season with a knee injury. The son of former cricketer, footballer and cricket umpire Barrie Meyer, Adie recovered to play the whole of the 1993/94 season before quitting the game.

Ray McHale welcomes new signing Andy Toman on the beach at Scarborough in February 1993. It was one of the last signings McHale made – the following month he was axed as Boro boss after three and a half years in charge.

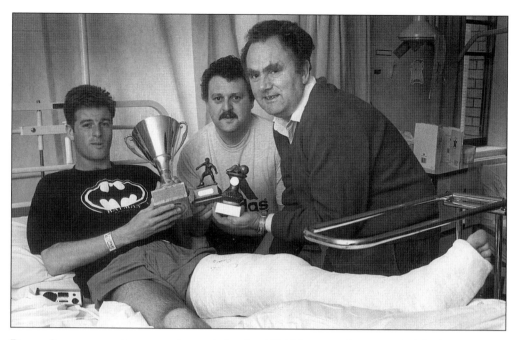

Darren Foreman receives several awards for the 1992/93 season from social club chairman Eric Pickup (right) and secretary Steve Mennell. Foreman hit 27 league goals during the season but suffered a broken leg during the final game against Carlisle United.

Phil Chambers (left), moved up from assistant to become Scarborough manager following the dismissal of Ray McHale. Working on a shoestring budget, he saw his side struggle badly during the early period of the 1993/94 season. In October, former Chelsea defender Steve Wicks (right), was appointed as manager, with Chambers moving back down to the assistant's role.

Steve Wicks' first signing was veteran goalkeeper John Burridge on a non-contract basis. Burridge started his career at Workington in 1970 and Scarborough was his thirteenth club. Wicks soon turned the side's fortunes round, but at the start of the 1994/95 season he was sacked by new chairman John Russell in unexplained circumstances.

The 1994/95 season proved very turbulent. Steve Wicks' replacement, former Boro player Billy Ayre, only lasted until December before Ray McHale returned to the manager's chair. With Boro finishing twenty-first in Division Three, there were few bright spots but the signing of midfielder David D'Auria from Barry Town was one of them. Here he looks set to receive a yellow card during Boro's dismal 2-0 defeat by Exeter City on 4 February.

Jason White scooped the Scarborough Evening News Player of the Year award for 1995. Never afraid to take on opposition defenders, White scored 11 league goals in 1994/95.

Scarborough pulled off something of a transfer coup in the summer of 1995 when securing the services of former Leeds United striker Andy Ritchie. Boro chairman John Russell

(left) and manager Ray McHale (centre) welcome Ritchie to the McCain Stadium on 28 June 1995.

Jason Rockett leads the way during pre-season training for the 1995/96 season. Signed on a free transfer from Rotherham United in 1993, Rockett served Boro very well at the heart of the defence for five seasons before being forced to retire due to a troublesome knee injury.

Striker Neil Trebble (right), in action against York City in a pre-season friendly on 5 August 1995. Signed on a free from Preston North End, he never really made an impact in front of goal and moved on to Stevenage Borough in March 1996.

Experienced forward Don Page in action in the 2-2 draw against Hereford United on 16 September 1995. Page came to Scarborough towards the end of a long career and after scoring five goals by mid-October, he lost his touch in front of goal and spent the rest of the season in and out of the side.

Andy Ritchie showed plenty of nice touches for Scarborough, but could only manage 8 goals during the season. With Boro lacking a regular goalscorer, they struggled throughout 1995/96, spending nearly all season near the foot of the table.

Young fans storm the pitch after the last league game of the 1995/96 season, a 4-1 defeat by Scunthorpe United. Scarborough finished second bottom of the Football League for the second successive season, with Mitch Cook taking over from Ray McHale as team manager for the last few games of the season.

After two disastrous seasons, a complete overhaul was needed in players and management for the 1996/97 campaign. Former Norwich City assistant boss Mick Wadsworth was appointed as manager in the summer of 1996 and quickly set about building a squad capable of success.

Scarborough started the 1996/97 season playing bright, confident football. The side went unbeaten for the first six games of the season including a 3-2 (5-4 on aggregate) win over Hull City at the McCain Stadium on 3 September.

Scarborough repeated a 3-2 win over Hull City when the two sides met again in the league on 15 October. Boro director George Westwood (front row, third from left), invited the whole Scarborough lifeboat crew as guests to the game.

Gareth Williams tussles with veteran defender Brian Kilcline in Scarborough's 2-1 victory over Mansfield Town on 26 October. Boro's form stuttered badly over the next couple of months and they finished twelfth in Division Three but this was a vast improvement on the previous two seasons.

One of Mick Wadsworth's best signings was former Sunderland defender/midfielder Gary Bennett (left). Bennett was ever present in 1996/97 and chipped in with 9 goals.

Goalkeeper Kevin Martin, a product of the club's youth scheme, came on leaps and bounds under Mick Wadsworth's management. By the start of the 1997/98 season he made the number one jersey his own, proving a confident and agile 'keeper.

During excavation works for the building of new stadium gates in the summer of 1997, a Victorian bottle bearing the same name as Scarborough chairman John Russell was excavated. Flanking Russell are striker Liam Robinson (left) and defender John Kay.

Striker Neil Campbell (left), in action against Notts County on 27 September 1997 with colleague Jamie Mitchell looking on. By now Boro were very much the finished article and remained in the promotion hunt throughout the season.

Scarborough manager Mick Wadsworth (left), built a well-balanced team playing attractive football. Crowds were back up at the McCain Stadium and Boro looked real promotion material. Unfortunately the side suffered a heavy 7-2 aggregate defeat in the Division Three play-off semi-finals against Torquay United and it was to be downhill from there.

Six
Relegation and Resurgence

Boro fans run onto the pitch after Scarborough had drawn 1-1 with Peterborough in their Division Three match on 8 May 1999. Celebrations proved to be premature – Carlisle's injury-time winner in their game against Plymouth condemned Boro to relegation from the Football League.

Financial pressures meant that Scarborough's play-off winning side was dismantled for the 1998/99 season. Former Workington full-back Paddy Atkinson was one of several players brought on in free transfers. Here he challenges Lee Steele in the 2-0 win over Shrewsbury on 9 September.

A 2-1 win at Halifax on 1 May put Boro within an ace of avoiding the drop from Division Three, despite having been rooted to bottom spot for several weeks previously. Matthew Russell and Halifax's Jamie Paterson battle for the ball.

A Boro fan looks on anxiously during Scarborough's 1-1 draw with Peterborough on 8 May 1999. It was a far cry from the play-off twelve months earlier as Boro lost the Football League status they had held for nearly twelve years.

Programme for Scarborough's last Football League match – for the time being! – against Peterborough. Only a few hundred of these were printed and with many copies snapped up by dealers, it has become a highly-collectable item.

On 14 August 1999 it was back to business for Scarborough in the Nationwide Conference. They kicked off in impressive fashion with a 5-0 win over Yeovil Town but in the end had to settle for a finishing position of fourth.

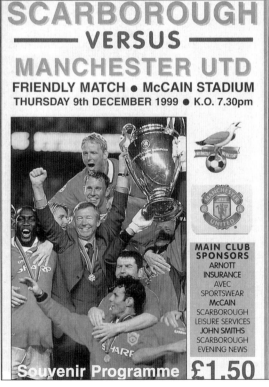

On 9 December 1999 Scarborough entertained Manchester United in a friendly match at the McCain Stadium. The fixture came about as a result of United's signing of Boro's Under-16 goalkeeper James Jowsey.

After finishing tenth in the Nationwide Conference in 2000/01, Scarborough began the 2001/02 campaign under severe financial strain. Youth team coach Ian Kerr was drafted in as first team boss and struggled to lift a scratch squad. Kerr holds his head in his hands as Boro crash out of the FA Cup to Unibond League side Whitby Town on 27 October.

With Boro bottom of the Nationwide Conference and facing possible extinction, a consortium headed by Malcolm Reynolds saved the club at the eleventh hour in November 2001. Reynolds brought in Russell Slade as manager and the team prospered. Here David Pounder hammers home Boro's opener in a convincing 2-0 win over eventual champions Boston United on 16 April 2002.

The team that Russ built. Russell Slade made a clutch of signings and took a revitalised Boro out of the drop zone in 2002. From left to right, back row: Brian Hodgson (kit man), Paul Shepherd, Karl Rose, Steve Baker, Shaun Rennison, Russell Slade (manager), Greg Shannon,

Darryn Stamp, Romain Faure, Ryan Sugden, Paul Atkinson, Mark Patterson. Front row: Mick Tarmey (physiotherapist), Phil Salt, Gareth Stoker, Danny Brunton, Scott Jordan, Jason Blunt, Mark Hotte, David Pounder, Darren Connell, Adam Jewell, Ian Kerr (youth team coach).

Scarborough players do a lap of honour after their last home game of 2001/02, a 0-0 draw against Dagenham and Redbridge on 24 April. Boro lost just two league matches in 2002 and shot up from bottom place to a finishing position of twelfth in the Nationwide Conference. For the first time in several years, the future looked bright for Scarborough Football Club.